ISBN 978-1-334-55454-4
PIBN 10656494

UNIVERSITY OF ILLINOIS

Agricultural Experiment Station.

URBANA, AUGUST, 1903.

BULLETIN No. 88.

SOIL TREATMENT FOR WHEAT IN ROTA-
TIONS, WITH SPECIAL REFERENCE
TO SOUTHERN ILLINOIS SOILS.

BY CYRIL G. HOPKINS, PH. D., CHIEF IN AGRONOMY AND CHEMISTRY.

In connection with the investigation of Illinois soils, the University of Illinois is conducting soil experiment fields on the most important types of soil in different sections of the state. The object of these experiments is to determine the best methods of soil treatment and the most suitable rotations for maintaining and increasing the productive capacity of Illinois soils. These soil experiment fields have been in operation only two years, but some results already obtained are so suggestive that it is believed they will be of value to the farmers and land owners of Illinois, and for that reason this preliminary bulletin is published at this time, giving results obtained with various kinds of soil treatment for wheat grown in rotations. It should be definitely understood that the soil treatment and rotations which we are trying must be followed for six or eight years at least before final conclusions can be drawn, whereas we have obtained only two years' results, not having had time as yet to complete even a three-year rotation.

PLAN OF EXPERIMENTS.

The plan of the rotations which we have adopted includes a liberal use of legumes (clover, cow peas, soy beans, vetch, etc.), both as catch crops and as regular crops in the rotation, but the 1902 crops were the first we have grown upon these soil experiment fields, and, of course, the wheat grown that year preceded the leguminous catch crops and received no benefit from them. In 1903 the wheat on certain plots followed either a regular crop or a catch crop of legumes, grown in 1902.

Our regular three-year rotation is as follows:

First year—Corn or wheat (with a legume catch crop on certain plots).

Second year—Oats (with a legume catch crop on the same plots as in the first year).

Third year—Legume (clover, cow peas, or some other legume).

All legume catch crops are plowed under for the benefit of the land. (Wherever practicable they may be pastured off.)

For a catch crop with corn, cow peas or soy beans are seeded between the rows when the corn is laid by, about the first of July; or winter vetch may be seeded with the cow peas or soy beans or it may be seeded alone when the corn is laid by, or at any time during July or August. The cow peas or soy beans usually grow rapidly until frost, while the vetch grows much more slowly at first, but continues to grow during the fall and again the next spring. In favorable seasons clover may be seeded in the corn when it is laid by to serve as a catch crop.

For a catch crop with wheat or oats, clover may be seeded in the spring or cow peas, soy beans, or winter vetch may be seeded as soon as possible after the wheat or oats is harvested, the stubble ground being either disked or preferably plowed, before seeding the catch crop.

The regular legume crop is usually all harvested and removed from the land, but on land which is very deficient in nitrogen this full crop of legumes may be plowed under on the same plots upon which legume catch crops are grown.

A regular four-year rotation may be:

    Corn, corn, oats and legume, or

    corn, oats, wheat and legume, or

    wheat, wheat, oats and legume.

A five-year rotation would be the same as a four-year rotation except that it would include one more crop of corn or wheat, or one of timothy.

In all rotations certain plots are seeded with legume catch crops every year. When a legume catch crop is grown or when the regular full crop of legumes on any plot is plowed under, it is termed "legume treatment." It is not called "legume treatment" when a full crop of legumes is grown and the entire crop removed from the land, as is usually done one year in all rotations.

Where lime is applied the amount used is governed by the need of the soil as ascertained by a determination of the soil acidity. On some soils the first application must be heavy, sometimes amounting to several tons, but afterward an application of 1,000 or 2,000 pounds once in six or eight years will probably be sufficient to keep the soil sweet.

Where phosphorus is applied, the regular plan is to apply 400 pounds of fine ground steamed bone meal the first year and afterwards 200 pounds a year. (On some fields, instead of 400 or 200 pounds of bone meal, we use 1,000 or 500 pounds, respectively, of ground rock phosphate.)

Where potassium is applied, the plan is to apply 200 pounds of potassium chlorid ("muriate" of potash), or 200 pounds of potassium sulfate the first year, and afterward 100 pounds a year.

On some of the fields, farm manure is also applied to certain plots, not only alone, but also in various combinations with other fertilizers. Where manure is applied, the regular plan is to apply it at the rate of two tons per acre per annum, but it is applied only once in a rotation. Thus, in a three-year rotation of corn, oats, and clover the manure would be applied at the rate of six tons per acre for the corn crop only. In a four-year rotation, eight tons per acre would be applied once in four years.

Attention is called to the fact that in considering yields from field experiments some allowance must be made for the natural variation which may exist between different plots. Very great care was taken in locating these soil experiment fields to select uniform land and our regular rule is to use the best land for the check plots (plots with no treatment) in case there is any indication of soil variation in the field. This is done in order that the results obtained by soil treatment shall not be exaggerated.

In this connection I have great pleasure in expressing my sincere appreciation of the faithful care and patience of the progressive farmers upon whose farms our soil experiment fields are located, who have had immediate charge of the regular work in carrying on these soil experiments. Their names are mentioned in connection with the descriptions of the individual fields.

Especial credit is due to my field assistant in soil experiments, Mr. J. E. Readhimer, who has superintended all of these fields, and has taken immediate charge of all operations not included in ordinary farm work, such as applying the different elements of plant food to the proper individual plots, taking exact yields of crops produced, and other unusual work.

(For more complete information regarding the different elements of plant food, the amounts required by different crops, and the purchase, use, and application of fertilizers, and for descriptions of the different soil areas in the state, the reader is referred to Illinois Experiment Station Circular No. 68, "Methods of Maintaining the Productive Capacity of Illinois Soils," which will be sent upon request to any farmer or land owner in the state.)

VIENNA SOIL EXPERIMENT FIELD.

This experiment field is located in the N. E. 10, N. E. 40, N. E. ¼, Sec. 9, Twp. 13 S., R. 3 E. of 3d P. M., on the farm of Mr. J.M. Price, near Vienna, Johnson County, on soil which is believed to be fairly representative of the common so-called "red clay" hill soil, the principal type in the unglaciated area, which includes the seven southernmost counties in the state.

This experiment field consists of fifteen fifth-acre plots arranged in three series of five plots each, numbered from 1 to 5.

The rotation for this field is:

First Year—Corn or wheat (with a legume catch crop on plots 2, 3, 4, and 5).

Second Year—Oats (with a legume catch crop on plots 2, 3, 4, and 5).

Third Year.—Legume (clover, cow peas, soy beans, or some other legume).

All regular crops in the rotation are grown every year; thus, one series of five plots may grow wheat, the next series oats, and the third series cow peas. The following year wheat would follow the cow peas, oats follow the wheat, and cow peas would be seeded on the series which had grown oats. Thus every crop is grown every year, which would not be the case if we made use of only one series of plots growing wheat one year, oats the next, and cow peas the next. The soil treatment is the same for each series. Plot No. 1 (in each series) receives no soil treatment, plot No. 2 receives the legume treatment; plot No. 3 legume treatment and lime; plot No. 4 legume treatment with lime and phosphorus; and plot No. 5 legume treatment with lime, phosphorus, and potassium. Thus lime is applied to plots 3, 4, and 5; phosphorus to plots 4 and 5; and potassium is applied to plot 5 only.

Wheat was not grown on the Vienna field in 1902, but in 1903 it was grown on one series of five plots. These plots had grown a regular crop of cow peas in 1902 and on plots 2, 3, 4, and 5, this legume crop had been plowed under.

Table 1 shows the kinds of treatment applied to the different plots and the yields of wheat obtained in 1903.

TABLE 1.—CROP YIELDS IN SOIL EXPERIMENTS; VIENNA FIELD.

Soil plot No.	Soil treatment applied* to "Red Clay" hill soil of the unglaciated area.	Bushels per acre, wheat, 1903
1	None	0.4†
	Legume	0.5†
	Legume, lime	0.7†
	Legume, lime, phosphorus	8.0
5	Legume, lime, phosphorus, potassium	11.0

* Only a part of the lime was applied before growing the 1902 crop; the rest after that crop was harvested.

† The yields for these three plots were estimated (see Table 2).

The wheat was practically a total failure on the three plots which had received no phosphorus, although a crop of legumes had been turned under on plot 2 and legumes with lime on plot 3.

Plot 4 which received phosphorus, with legume treatment and lime, yielded eight bushels per acre; and plot 5, which received legume treatment with lime, phosphorus, and potassium, yielded eleven bushels.

Of course the season was considered exceptionally unfavorable for wheat, otherwise a small crop at least would have been obtained on the untreated plot. Many large fields of wheat in the vicinity of Vienna were practically failures, several farmers reporting yields no greater than the seed which had been sown.

ODIN SOIL EXPERIMENT FIELD.

This experiment field is located chiefly in the S. W. 40, S. W. ¼, Sec. 14, Twp. 2 N., R. 1 E. of 3d P. M., on the farm of Col. N. B. Morrison, near Odin, Marion County, on the ordinary gray silt soil (commonly called "white clay" soil) of the lower Illinoisan glaciation, a soil area which includes more or less of about twenty-five counties in South Central Illinois.

This experiment field consists of forty fifth-acre plots arranged in four series of ten plots each, five of each series of ten plots being tile-drained and the other five not tile-drained. (Four-inch tile are laid about three and a half feet deep and five rods apart, one string through the center of each drained plot.)

Wheat was not grown on this field in 1902, but in 1903 it was grown in the one series upon plots which had grown oats in 1902, the oats having been followed by a catch crop of cow peas on certain plots as indicated in Table 2, which shows the kinds of treatment applied to the different plots and the yields of oats obtained in 1902 and of wheat obtained in 1903.

TABLE 2.—CROP YIELDS IN SOIL EXPERIMENTS; ODIN FIELD.

Soil plot No.	Soil treatment applied * to gray silt soil of the lower Illinois glaciation.	Bushels per acre.	
		Not tile-drained.	Tile-drained.
OATS, 1902.			
1	None	15.8	12.2
2	Legume	16.1	10.3
3	Legume, lime	14.1	11.7
4	Legume, lime, phosphorus	16.7	19.2
5	Legume, lime, phosphorus, potassium	18.8	17.7
WHEAT, 1903.			
1	None	0.4†	0.5†
2	Legume	0.5†	0.6†
3	Legume, lime	0.7†	2.1†
4	Legume, lime, phosphorus	5.8	13.4
5	Legume, lime, phosphorus, potassium	14.0	15.2

* The legume treatment applies only to the crop yields for 1903, and only a part of the lime was applied before the 1902 crop was grown.

† The sheaves, or bundles, from each of these six very low yielding plots were counted separately, but the wheat from the six plots was all threshed as one lot, and the weights then apportioned among the different plots as indicated by the number of bundles. The yields from the first three lots on the Vienna Field were estimated to be the same as from the corresponding untiled Odin plots. All other yields given are actual weights.

PLATE 1.—WHEAT CROP WITH NO TREATMENT: ODIN SOIL EXPERIMENT FIELD.

Plates 1, 2, and 3 show the condition of several of the wheat plots just before they were harvested.

Plate 1 is from a photograph of the tile-drained plot No. 1, which had

PLATE 2.—WHEAT CROP WITH LEGUME AND LIME TREATMENT: ODIN SOIL EXPERIMENT FIELD.

PLATE 3.—WHEAT CROP WITH LEGUME, LIME, AND PHOSPHORUS TREATMENT:
ODIN SOIL EXPERIMENT FIELD.

received no special soil treatment and which yielded 0.5 bushels of wheat per acre.

Plate 2 shows the condition of the wheat on the tile-drained plot No. 3 which received lime and on which a catch crop of cow peas had been turned under.   It yielded 2.1 bushels of wheat per acre.

Plate 3 shows the wheat on the tile-drained plot No. 4, which received lime, phosphorus and legume treatment.   It yielded 13.4 bushels of wheat, or 11.3 bushels more than plot No. 3, the increase apparently due to the application of phosphorus.

It will be observed that the tile-drained plot No. 4 (legume, lime, phosphorus), produced a noticeably higher yield of both oats and wheat than the corresponding undrained plot, the difference in yield being 2.5 bushels of oats and 7.6 bushels of wheat in favor of the drained plot. On the other hand, on the first three plots the tile-drained land gives smaller yields of oats and only slightly larger yields of wheat than the undrained land.

CUTLER SOIL EXPERIMENT FIELD.

This experiment field is located chiefly in the N. 20, S. E. 40, N. W. ¼, Sec. 19, Twp. 5 S., R. 4 W. of 3d P. M., on the farm of Mr. W. E. Braden about five miles northwest of Cutler, on the line between Perry and Randolph counties, on the so-called "white clay"* (gray silt) soil of the lower

---

* This soil is not clay, but largely silt.   It might be called a *gray silt loam;* it is a fine friable powder (finer than sand) ; but it is not plastic clay.

Illinoisan glaciation, but the soil at Cutler is perhaps a slightly better phase of this type than that at Odin.

The rotation experiments occupy thirty fifth-acre plots arranged in three divisions of ten plots each. Wheat was grown on ten plots in 1902. The results obtained are given in Table 3.

TABLE 3.—CROP YIELDS IN SOIL EXPERIMENTS; CUTLER FIELD

Soil plot No.	Soil treatment applied to gray silt soil in the lower Illinoisan glaciation.	Bushels per acre, wheat, 1902.
1	None	12.8
2	None	12.4
3	None	12.4
4	None	13.3
5	None	12.9
6	Phosphorus	16.9
7	Phosphorus	16.1
8	Phosphorus, potassium	20.8
9	Phosphorus, potassium	19.4
10	Phosphorus, potassium	20.8

In 1903 wheat was grown on ten plots which had grown a regular crop of cow peas in 1902. On plots 2, 4, 6, and 8 the cow peas were turned under ("legume treatment"); but on the other plots the crop of cow peas was harvested and removed. On plots 3, 5, 7, and 9 an application of farm manure was made to the cow-pea stubble ground, which was then plowed for wheat. Table 4 shows the results obtained in 1903.

TABLE 4.—CROP YIELDS IN SOIL EXPERIMENTS; CUTLER FIELD.

Soil plot No.	Soil treatment applied to gray silt soil in the lower Illinoisan glaciation.	Bushels per acre, wheat, 1903
1	None	6.0
2	Legume	9.2
3	Manure	12.1
4	Legume, lime	13.5
5	Manure, lime	13.3
6	Legume, lime, phosphorus	20.3
7	Manure, lime, phosphorus	20.8
8	Legume, lime, phosphorus, potassium	26.8
9	Manure, lime, phosphorus, potassium	24.0
10	Lime, phosphorus, potassium	21.1

The yields of wheat obtained from the crops of 1902 and 1903 on the Cutler experiment field certainly show very markedly the effect of applications of plant food.

In 1902 there were five plots which received no treatment and the yields from those five plots were exceedingly uniform, varying from 12.4 to 13.3 bushels. Phosphorus gave an increase of about 4 bushels. and both phosphorus and potassium an increase of about eight bushels, above. the yields from the untreated plots.

In 1903 the yield on the untreated plot was six bushels. Where cow peas had been turned under the yield was increased by 3.2 bushels, and where lime was applied and cow peas turned under the increase was 7.5 bushels over the untreated plot, making a yield of 13.5 bushels. Legume, lime, and phosphorus gave a yield of 20.3 bushels, an increase of 14.3 bushels over the untreated plot; and with legume, lime, phosphorus, and potassium the total yield was 26.8 bushels of wheat, making a net increase of 20.8 bushels over the untreated plot.

Manure produced almost the same effect as turning under cow peas, except that when no other treatment was added the manure gave 2.9 bushels better yield than the legume treatment, whereas, when all other treatments were added (plots 208 and 209), the legume gave 2.8 bushels better yield than the manure.

Where lime, phosphorus, and potassium were applied without legume or manure (plot 210) the yield was 21.1 bushels, which is 15.1 bushels more than the untreated plot, but 5.7 bushels less than where cow peas were turned under, and 2.9 bushels less than where manure was used with applications of lime, phosphorus and potassium.

It is probable that the legume supplies more nitrogen (gathered from the air) than the manure, but the manure adds to the soil a small amount of phosphorus and a considerable quantity of potassium, while the legume supplies no phosphorus or potassium except what it takes from the soil in growing.

PLATE 4.—WHEAT CROP WITH NO TREATMENT: CUTLER SOIL EXPERIMENT FIELD.

Plate 4 shows the wheat crop on the untreated plot No. 1; and Plate 5 shows plot No. 6 (legume, lime, phosphorus) on the left, and plot No. 7 (manure, lime, phosphorus) on the right; also in the center, between the plots, an untreated half-rod division strip.

MASCOUTAH SOIL EXPERIMENT FIELD.

This experiment field is located in the S. 20, S. W. 40, S. E. ¼, Sec. 17, Twp. 1 N., R. 6 W. of 3d P. M., on the farm of Mr. George Postel (operated by Mr. John A. Rumer), about three miles north of Mascoutah, St. Clair County, on the brown silt soil of the middle Illinoisan glaciation.

This soil in St. Clair County is evidently a somewhat lighter phase of the type than is found farther north. (This is the principal type of soil in Sangamon and adjoining counties, but in St. Clair County the soil is somewhat older and more worn.)

The rotation experiments on this field occupy forty tenth-acre plots, arranged in four series of ten plots each. The rotation followed thus far is corn, oats, wheat, and cow peas, with legume catch crops on certain plots with or after the corn, oats, and wheat.

PLATE 5.—WHEAT CROP WITH NO TREATMENT IN THE CENTER, WITH LEGUME, LIME, PHOSPHORUS ON THE LEFT, AND WITH MANURE, LIME, PHOSPHORUS ON THE RIGHT: CUTLER SOIL EXPERIMENT FIELD.

In 1902, the results obtained with wheat were as shown in Table 5.

TABLE 5.—CROP YIELDS IN SOIL EXPERIMENTS; MASCOUTAH FIELD.

Soil plot No.	Soil treatment applied* to brown silt soil of the middle Illinoisan glaciation.	Bushels per acre, wheat, 1902.
1	None	19.7
2	None	15.2
3	None	15.3
4	Lime	17.7
5	Lime	16.5
6	Lime, phosphorus	24.7
7	Lime, phosphorus	28.0
8	Lime, phosphorus, potassium	29.8
9	Lime, phosphorus, potassium	31.7
10	Lime, phosphorus, potassium	39.8

* Only part of the lime was applied before growing the 1902 crop.

These results show very markedly the effect of phosphorus, the yield of wheat having been increased by that element from about sixteen bushels to twenty-six bushels. Where potassium was applied there was a farther increase, but the results are quite discordant from plots treated alike, indicating some soil differences.

In 1903 wheat was grown on plots which had grown oats in 1902, a catch crop of cow peas (seeded on the stubble ground), having been grown after the oats on certain plots ("legume treatment"). The ground was plowed for wheat about September 20, 1902, and the wheat seeded soon afterward. The weather conditions which followed proved very unfavorable for wheat seeded on late plowing, and the early seeded wheat was badly injured by the Hessian fly; consequently the 1903 wheat crop on these plots was practically a failure—very much poorer than on adjoining land which had been plowed early in the fall. The results obtained are of little value and if not understood would be misleading as to the effect of the different kinds of soil treatment. Table 6 gives the yields of oats in 1902, and of wheat in 1903, obtained on these plots.

TABLE 6.—CROP YIELDS IN SOIL EXPERIMENTS; MASCOUTAH FIELD.

Soil plot No.	Soil treatment applied* to brown silt loam of the middle Illinoisan glaciation.	Bushels per acre.	
		Oats, 1902.	Wheat, 1903.
1	None	31.6	4.7
2	Legume	37.2	5.0
3	None	41.6	4.8
4	Legume, lime	43.8	7.5
5	Lime	45.0	4.3
6	Legume, lime, phosphorus	46.9	10.5
7	Lime, phosphorus	46.3	4.7
8	Legume, lime, phosphorus, potassium	50.6	8.0
9	Lime, phosphorus, potassium	54.1	6.5
10	Lime, phosphorus, potassium	57.8	7.4

* Only part of the lime was applied before growing the 1902 crop, and the legume treatment applies only to the 1903 crop yields.

Of course no conclusions regarding soil treatment can be drawn from the 1903 wheat yields on these plots, unless possibly that there is an indication of some slight benefit from the "legume" treatment, especially in connection with phosphorus.

GENERAL DISCUSSION OF RESULTS.

The tables in the foregoing pages give all of the results which we have obtained in 1902 and 1903, with different kinds of soil treatment for wheat grown in rotations upon the regular University soil experiment fields, located in different sections of southern Illinois. They show some discrepancies which are not explained by the differences in soil treatment, but which may be due to variations in the original condition of the different plots, or in some cases, possibly to differences in the amount of injury caused by the Hessian fly, chinch bug or other insects, which cannot usually be ascertained with accuracy. With the exception of the very poor 1903 wheat crop on the Mascoutah field, the results in general are a trustworthy index of the effect of the soil treatment.

The Cutler field is on very uniform soil and the results obtained on that field may well serve as the basis for a general discussion of the effects of soil treatment. While the results in 1902 were much more marked on the Mascoutah field, they were more discordant and relatively less reliable than those at Cutler. The Cutler field includes practically the same kinds of experiments which have been conducted at Vienna, at Odin, and at Mascoutah; and, in addition, the manure treatment was applied at Cutler for the 1903 wheat crop.

During the two years about three tons of slacked lime, 600 pounds of bone meal (containing about 13 percent of phosphorus, or seventy-eight pounds of that element), and 300 pounds of potassium sulfate* (containing about 40 *percent of potassium*, or 120 pounds of that element) have been applied per acre on the proper plots at Cutler. On certain plots sixteen tons of farm manure were applied per acre in the fall of 1902. (This was a heavier application than it was intended to have applied, twelve tons being sufficient for six years, or six tons for three years, on the basis that two tons of manure per acre per annum is as much manure as a stock farmer can produce from the crops grown on his own farm.) Cow peas were grown in 1902, and on certain plots the entire crop was plowed under in the fall.

It is not expected that it will be necessary to apply any more lime for at least five years, and after that time probably 1,000 pounds of lime per acre once in five to ten years will be sufficient to keep the soil free from acidity and in suitable condition for growing legumes. After we have grown a legume catch crop for one rotation we do not expect to plow under the regular legume crop on any of the plots, but to depend upon the

*The chlorid was used one year in place of the sulfate.

legume catch crop, and the stubble and roots of the legume used in the regular rotation, to maintain the supply of nitrogen.

The question naturally and necessarily arises whether any of these different kinds of soil treatment will prove to be profitable; and, if so, which treatment is likely to be the most profitable. While the experiments have been in progress only two years and of course no final conclusions can be drawn, yet some computations can easily be made which may be of value even though they are somewhat tentative.

The yield of wheat on the untreated plot was six bushels per acre. At 60 cents a bushel this amounts to $3.60. Assuming the farm to be worth $40 an acre, the investment at 5 percent would require $2.00 to pay the interest. This would leave a balance of $1.60 an acre to pay for raising the wheat. But even this amount, $1.60, is too high, unless the soil which grows the crop contains an unfailing supply of plant food, which is certainly not the case with the principal type of soil in the lower Illinoisan glaciation. By reference to Table 1, page 4, of our Circular No. 68, "Methods of Maintaining the Productive Capacity of Illinois Soils" (which will be sent upon request to any Illinois farmer or land owner), it will be seen that a six-bushel crop of wheat would remove from the soil about ten pounds of nitrogen, one and two-thirds pounds of phosphorus and seven pounds of potassium. That these elements of plant food actually possesses an agricultural value in this soil is well demonstrated by the crop yields from this field as shown in Tables 3 and 4. For example, we have applied during the two years 600 pounds of bone meal per acre to certain plots on this field. The bone meal contains 13 percent of the element phosphorus, or thirteen pounds per hundred, making a total of seventy-eight pounds of phosphorus applied. The first year phosphorus increased the yield of wheat from 12.8 bushels to 16.5 bushels, making an increase of 3.7 bushels of wheat. The second year the phosphorus increased the yield from 13.4 to 20.6 bushels, or 7.2 bushels increase, making a total increase of 10.9 bushels for the two years. At 60 cents a bushel, this increase of 10.9 bushels would have a value of $6.54. Dividing this amount by seventy-eight we find that the phosphorus has already paid back in wheat more than eight cents a pound for every pound applied. When we bear in mind that the increase of 10.9 bushels has removed from the soil only three pounds of phosphorus and that we have seventy-five pounds of the phosphorus applied still left in the soil to benefit succeeding crops, we can then appreciate the fact that phosphorus has an agricultural value in this soil.

Now, what is the value of these different elements of plant food, nitrogen, phosphorus, and potassium? They may be valued in two different ways.

First. They have a commercial value. The commercial value is what it costs to get them.

Second. They have an agricultural value. The agricultural value is measured by the increased crop yields which they give when applied to the soil.

These two different values are almost independent of each other. The commercial value varies with the cost of preparation, grinding, transportation, etc., while the agricultural value varies with the character and composition of the soil to which the plant food is applied, also with the kind of crop to be grown.

To illustrate, dried blood, which contains 14 percent of nitrogen, costs about $42 a ton, wholesale in Chicago. Thus, 280 pounds of the element nitrogen bought in this form would cost $42, or 15 cents a pound; and this is the commercial value of nitrogen in dried blood. The nitrogen in dried blood is practically all available for the use of plants.

We have applied dried blood on several soil experiment fields located on various types of soil in different sections of Illinois. While our data are not yet sufficient to warrant final conclusions, I may say that thus far the results from these field experiments have given the nitrogen in dried blood an agricultural value varying from zero to about 2 cents a pound, measured by the increase in crop yields produced.

By reference to Table 6, page 24, of Circular 68, it will be seen that the results of ten years' investigations by the Ohio Experiment Station show the agricultural value of nitrogen applied to be from 1.2 cents to 9.1 cents a pound, while the cost or commercial value was at least 15 cents a pound.

All of these results refer to the use of commercial nitrogen in general farming. Of course, in market gardening or in other intensive farming upon land of very high value, and where crops of high value are produced on an acre of land, and especially in the forcing of early vegetables in order to obtain the highest price in the early part of the season, the agricultural value of nitrogen may sometimes amount to many times its cost. Such lands are usually far too valuable to give them up to the growing of legumes even for a part of the season.

The New Jersey Experiment Station has recently shown that the application of 300 pounds of nitrate of soda per acre, costing $6.75, increased the value of the celery crop from $118.30 to $381.90 per acre. This was due in part to increased yield, but much more largely to improvement in the quality of the crop produced. It is also very probable that nitrogen could be used with profit on permanent meadow lands near the large markets in the eastern and southern states where the hay can be sold directly for a maximum price, with little or no expense for transportation.

On the other hand, the general farmer not only cannot afford to purchase commercial nitrogen, but there is absolutely no necessity whatever for him to do so. The air is about four-fifths nitrogen, and as the atmos-

PLATE 6.—TRIPLICATE TEST OF THE EFFECT OF ALFALFA BACTERIA IN GROWING ALFALFA IN ORDINARY FARM SOILS WITHOUT FERTILIZERS—JARS MARKED "BAC." CONTAIN ALFALFA BACTERIA.

pheric pressure amounts to about fifteen pounds to the square inch, there are actually nearly twelve pounds of nitrogen resting upon every square inch of the earth's surface, and although ordinary agricultural plants have no power to feed upon this free nitrogen of the air (being dependent upon the combined nitrogen in the soil for their supply), we now know that by means of the different species of nitrogen-gathering bacteria which inhabit or should inhabit the roots of different legumes, nitrogen can be obtained from this free and inexhaustible supply of the atmosphere for about 1 cent a pound. Thus, for example, we can sow red clover in the wheat, oats, or rye for less than $1 an acre and grow a crop of clover containing more than 100 pounds of nitrogen an acre. We can also accomplish this result with a catch crop of cow peas, soy beans, or vetch, and probably with crimson clover or alfalfa after our soils become thoroughly infected with the proper bacteria. Exact investigations have shown that alfalfa properly infected with the alfalfa bacteria obtains practically all of its nitrogen from the air, even when grown on the black prairie soils of central Illinois.

The alfalfa grown in pots 37, 47, and 48, Plate 6, obtained about 90 percent of its total nitrogen content from the air. (All of these pots were filled with ordinary Illinois black prairie soil, which had been thoroughly mixed before the pots were filled. The only difference among the six pots is that alfalfa bacteria were added to the three pots marked "Bac.," thus enabling the alfalfa in those pots to obtain nitrogen from the air. Our Bulletin No. 76, "Alfalfa on Illinois Soil," will be sent upon request to any Illinois farmer or land owner who may be interested in alfalfa.) We have also found that the poorer the soil the greater is the proportion of nitrogen taken from the air, as compared with that taken from the soil.

In this connection it may be well to call attention to the fact that it is not necessary to apply any nitrogen to the soil in order to enable legumes to start growing. We have obtained a good stand and luxuriant growth of legumes in a soil which was absolutely free of nitrogen, simply by providing suitable conditions, including a sufficient supply of the mineral elements of plant food (as phosphorus and potassium), lime, if needed, and thorough inocculation with the proper species of nitrogen-gathering bacteria.

What then is the commercial value of nitrogen? Manifestly, what it costs to get it. In general farming it is probably safe to say 1 cent a pound—for nitrogen already delivered and spread over the ground.

The commercial value of phosphorus varies with the form in which it is purchased. Ground rock phosphate, containing at least 12 to 13 percent of the element phosphorus, can be bought in carload lots for $7 to $8 a ton delivered at almost any point in Illinois. This amounts to say $7.50 for 250 pounds of phosphorus, or 3 cents a pound for the element. Fine ground steamed bone meal containing 12 to 13 percent of phosphorus can be bought delivered at any railway station in the state for $25 to $30 a ton. In this form the phosphorus costs about 12 cents a pound. Aside from ground rock phosphate, the steamed bone meal is the cheapest form of phosphorus on the market. The bone meal is known to be a very satisfactory form of phosphorus to use and the results of our experiments with it prove that it acts readily as a source of phosphorus for wheat. It has not been treated with acid and is suitable for use on any soil in the State which needs phosphorus. As stated in Circular No. 68, pages 16 and 17, some experiments have been conducted (and are still in progress), which strongly indicate that, for equal amounts of money invested in ground rock phosphate and bone meal, the ground rock phosphate will give about as good immediate results when applied in connection with a liberal use of legumes or farm manure, and will be more lasting in its effect, than the bone meal. On the other hand, it would have practically no agricultural value if applied to a soil exceedingly deficient in organic matter unless accompanied by an application of farm manure or a liberal use of legumes.

The commercial value of the element potassium is about 6 cents a pound. The cheapest form of potassium is potassium chlorid, which contains about 42 percent of this element and costs about $50 a ton. (See Circular No. 68 for more complete explanations regarding the elements of plant food, how and where they can be obtained, methods of application, etc.)

Returning to the discussion of the yield of wheat from the untreated plot on the Cutler Soil Experiment Field, it will be seen by reference to Table 1, page 4, of Circular No. 68, that six bushels of wheat and accompanying straw would remove from the soil about ten pounds of nitrogen, one and two-thirds pounds of phosphorus and seven pounds of potassium. Allowing 1 cent for nitrogen, 3 cents for phosphorus and 6 cents for potassium as the commerical value of these elements, the six-bushel crop of wheat would remove 10 cents worth of nitrogen, 5 cents worth of phosphorus and 42 cents worth of potassium from the soil, making a total of 57 cents from an acre. If we consider the commercial value of phosphorus as 12 cents a pound, as it is in bone meal. then we have removed 20 cents worth of phosphorus or 72 cents worth of the three elements. We shall certainly be within safe limits to place phosphorus at 12 cents a pound, as it can be obtained in bone meal for that price. (Bone meal is a form of phosphorus which has been used for many years and it is known to be reliable and to give good results, consequently we are safe in basing our computation upon the price of phosphorus in bone meal, although it is believed that when used under proper conditions phosphorus in the form of ground rock phosphate will prove to be more economical.)

Plot No. 1: No treatment. If we allow $3.60 for the six bushels of wheat and then deduct $2 for interest on the investment and 72 cents for plant food removed from the soil, we have left 88 cents to pay for raising an acre of wheat.

Plot No 2: Legume treatment. This plot yielded 9.2 bushels per acre, which at 60 cents would amount to $5.52. The cost of seed and seeding for a catch crop of legumes is about $1 an acre, varying of course with the kind of seed and method of seeding. The commercial value or cost of replacing the plant food removed by a wheat crop yielding 9.2 bushels amounts to $1.10. Adding to this the cost of legume treatment and $2 for interest on the investment makes $4.10, leaving 1.42 cents to pay for raising an acre of wheat. (It may be stated that we have really allowed double pay for providing nitrogen, first by paying $1 for the legume treatment, second by charging 1 cent a pound for the fifteen pounds of nitrogen removed in the crop.)

Plot No. 3: Manure treatment. This plot yielded 12.1 bushels per acre, which at 60 cents a bushel would amount to $7.26. The value of the plant food removed by a wheat crop yielding 12.1 bushels amounts to $1.45, counting 1 cent for nitrogen, 12 cents for phosphorus, and 6 cents for potassium, per pound.

It is exceedingly difficult to estimate the cost of the manure treatment. If the farmer has the manure on hand he may consider that the only cost is the hauling and spreading. Even if he hires the work done this should not amount to more than 30 cents a ton or $4.80 for the sixteen tons which were applied. With $2 for interest, $1.45 for plant food removed, and $4.80 for the manure treatment, we have a total of $8.25 expense, or 99 cents more than the total value of the crop, which was $7.26. In other words, if we consider the first year only, we have lost 99 cents an acre besides the entire expense of raising an acre of wheat. This would make a poor showing indeed for the manure treatment; but we have here another factor to consider, namely, that the value of the manure is not exhausted with the first crop. In fact, it is usually of greater benefit to the second crop than to the first and continues to benefit succeeding crops for several years. (Attention is called to the fact that this is also true with legume crops to some extent, and in some cases even when the entire crop is removed, only the stubble and roots being left with the soil.)

By reference to Table 2, page 12, of our Circular No. 68, it will be seen that a ton of average farm manure contains ten pounds of nitrogen, two pounds of phosphorus, and ten pounds of potassium; or sixteen tons of manure would contain 160 pounds of nitrogen, 32 pounds of phosphorus, and 160 pounds of potassium. The fact that the effect of applying manure lasts for many years is evidence that the elements of plant food which it contains are not in a readily available form. The phosphorus in manure should be as valuable as that in ground rock phosphate, and probably the potassium in manure should be valued on about the same basis; that is, one-fourth as much as in a readily available form like potassium chlorid. With nitrogen at 1 cent, phosphorus at 3 cents, and potassium at $1\frac{1}{2}$ cents, manure would be worth 31 cents a ton, or $4.96 for the sixteen tons. There may be some question whether $1\frac{1}{2}$ cents a pound for the potassium in manure is a fair estimate. We believe that it is. By referring to Table 4, it will be seen that although the manure applied to plot 7 contained 160 pounds of potassium, most of it was not available for use of the crop, because where we added commercial potassium (plot 9) in connection with the manure the yield was increased from 20.8 to 24 bushels per acre.

Manure treatment should be considered as adding to the value of the land. If the untreated land is worth $40 an acre, it is worth $44.80 after sixteen tons of farm manure have been applied to it. The added plant food becomes a part of the permanent investment, I say *permanent* because it is about as permanent as the value of the land itself. In some places in the eastern states, land which was once worth $100 an acre or more is now worth $35. Why? Chiefly because valuable plant food has been sold off. A twenty-bushel wheat crop removes 82 cents worth of plant food, counting nitrogen at 1 cent, phosphorus at 3 cents, and potassium at $1\frac{1}{2}$ cents a pound. In seventy-five years this would amount to over $60 worth of plant food. This amount would practically cover the decrease in the value of the land. The farmers of southern Illinois are in a better position to appreciate these facts than those who are selling 60 bushels of corn a year off from the comparatively new and naturally rich black land in the north central part of the state.

Returning to the specific discussion of plot No. 3 (manure treatment), if we allow interest on $44.80, we only add 24 cents to the annual expense, aside from paying for the larger amount of plant food removed. On this basis plot No. 3 should be credited with 12.1 bushels at 60 cents, amounting to $7.26, and charged with $2.24 for interest and $1.45 for plant food removed. Deducting $3.69 from the total receipts leaves $3.57 to pay for raising an acre of wheat.

Plot No. 4: Legume, lime. This plot yielded 13.5 bushels of wheat worth $8.10. The cost of an application of slacked lime or ground limestone (one to two tons per acre), will amount to from $3 to $6 an acre, but to be safe, even for strongly acid soils, let us say $10 an acre. This is a direct investment and it must be added to the value of the land, making it $50 an acre. In addition to this it may be necessary to apply half a ton of ground limestone every five or six years to keep the soil free from acidity or we may say that 25 cents worth of lime per acre is destroyed each year by cropping. In this connection it may be said that ground rock phosphate contains large amounts of lime and other basic materials (usually some lime carbonate) and it is not improbable that moderate annual applications of ground rock phosphate will be quite sufficient to keep the soil free from acidity, after it has once been corrected by the initial application of lime.

With $2.50 for interest, $1 for legume treatment, and $1.87 for plant food removed by the crop (including the lime destroyed), we have a total of $5.37 to be deducted from $8.10 leaving a balance of $2.73 to pay for raising an acre of wheat.

Plot No. 5: Manure, lime. (The chief benefit of the lime on this plot will doubtless be for the growth of the legume in the regular rotation.) This plot yielded 13.3 bushels of wheat, worth $7.98. After deducting $2.74 for interest and $1.85 for plant food removed, we have left $3.39 to pay for raising an acre of wheat.

Plot No. 6: Legume, lime, phosphorus. This plot yielded 20.3 bushels of wheat in 1903, but we must also credit this plot with the increase of 3.7 bushels which this treatment (or the phosphorus alone) produced in 1902. This makes a total credit of twenty-four bushels, worth $14.40. The seventy-eight pounds of phosphorus applied would cost $9.36 at 12 cents a pound. This must be added to the value of the land, making the total value $59.36. With $2.97 for interest, $1 for legume treatment, and $3.13 for plant food removed, we have $7.10 to be deducted from $14.40, leaving a balance of $7.30 to pay for raising an acre of wheat.

Plot No. 7: Manure, lime, phosphorus. This plot yielded 20.8 bushels of wheat. Adding the increase of 3.7 bushels produced by the phosphorus applied for the 1902 crop, we have 24.5 bushels worth $14.70. Deducting $3.21 for interest and $3.19 for plant food removed, we have left $8.30 to pay for raising an acre of wheat.

Plot No. 8: Legume, lime, phosphorus, potassium. This plot yielded 26.8 bushels in 1903. Adding the increase of 7.5 bushels produced by the phosphorus and potassium in 1902, we have 34.3 bushels of wheat, worth $20.58. The 120 pounds of potassium applied to this plot at 6 cents a pound make $7.20, which must be added to the value of the land, making the total value $66.56 an acre. With $3.33 for interest, $1 for legume treatment, and $4.37 for plant food removed, we have a total of $8.70 to be deducted from $20.58, leaving a balance of $11.88 to pay for raising an acre of wheat.

Plot No. 9: Manure, lime, phosphorus, potassium. This plot yielded twenty-four bushels. Adding the increase of 7.5 bushels from the 1902 crop makes 31.5 bushels worth $18.90. The cost of this land is now $40 for the untreated land, $4.80 for manure, $10 for lime, $9.36 for phosphorus, and $7.20 for potassium, making the total cost $71.36 an acre. With $3.57 for interest and $4.03 for plant food removed (including 25 cents for lime destroyed) amounting to $7.60 we have left from the $18.90 receipts a balance of $11.30 to pay for raising an acre of wheat.

TABLE 7.—RESULTS OF SOIL TREATMENT: CUTLER EXPERIMENT FIELD.

Soil plot No.	Soil treatment applied to gray silt loam of the lower Illinoisan glaciation.	Total cost of land per acre.	Expense statement.				Wheat obtained.		Received for raising an acre of wheat.
			Interest on investment.	Cost of legume treatment.	Value of plant food removed.	Expense per acre.	Bushels per acre.	Value per acre.	
201	None	$40.00	$2.00	.....	$0.72	$2.72	6.0	$3.60	$0.88
202	Legume	40.00	2.00	$1.00	1.10	4.10	9.2	5.52	1.42
203	Manure	44.80	2.24	.....	1.45	3.69	12.1	7.26	3.57
204	Legume, lime	50.00	2.50	1.00	1.87	5.37	13.5	8.10	2.73
205	Manure, lime	54.80	2.74	.....	1.85	4.59	13.3	7.98	3.39
206	Legume, lime, phosphorus	59.36	2.97	1.00	3.15	7.10	24.0	14.40	7.30
207	Manure, lime, phosphorus	64.16	3.21	.....	3.19	6.40	24.5	14.70	8.30
208	Legume, lime, phosphorus, potassium	66.56	3.33	1.00	4.37	8.70	34.3	20.58	11.88
209	Manure, lime, phosphorus, potassium	71.36	3.57	.....	4.03	7.60	31.5	18.90	11.30
210	lime, phosphorus, potassium	66.56	3.33	.....	3.68	7.01	28.6	17.16	10.15

Plot No. 10: Lime, phosphorus, potassium. This plot yielded 21.1 bushels, which with the 7.5 bushels increase from the previous year, makes 28.6 bushels, worth $17.16. Deducting $3.33 for interest and $3.68 for plant food removed, leaves a balance of $10.15 to pay for raising an acre of wheat.

Table 7 shows these data from the different plots in concise form for easy comparison.

Of course these computations might be somewhat modified for different conditions, depending upon distance of the farm from the railroad station, the price of wheat, the amount of lime required to correct the acidity of the soil, the amount of potassium found most profitable, etc., etc. It is believed that the estimates which have been made are on the safe side for the farmer. The expense of applying the manure, the lime, and the legume treatment has been included in the tabular statement, either in the investment (when the application lasts for many years) or in the annual expense (as with the legume treatment). The cost of the phosphorus and potassium is based upon well-recognized, trustworthy standard forms of those elements, allowing the full market price for them. No allowance has been made for the expense of applying those two elements, because there is practically no expense necessary. Even if both phosphorus and potassium are used, they can be applied at once by means of a fertilizer drill provided with fertilizer, grain, and grass-seed attachments, such as the Superior fertilizer disk drill. We have used this drill in this way and know that it can easily be done. Thus we can run bone meal through the force-feed grain box and run potassium chlorid through the regular fertilizer box, and at the same time we mix the fertilizers as they fall, probably more perfectly than any fertilizer manufacturer does or can do. Furthermore, we can make any brand of fertilizer we choose by simply varying the feed of the two boxes. Thus we can sow 200 pounds of bone meal and 100 pounds of potassium chlorid; or we can sow 300 pounds of bone meal and 50 pounds of potassium chlorid, or almost any other proportions we may desire.

If only one fertilizer is used, as bone meal, it can be run through the fertilizer box at the same time the seed is run through the grain box. By some people it is considered the best practice to drill the fertilizer one direction and then drill the grain crosswise. In this case both boxes could be used for fertilizers the first time over the ground. By using a disk drill the ground can be disked at the same time. There is no objection to sowing bone meal (raw, common, or steamed) or ground rock phosphate, or ground limestone through the fertilizer box at the same time as the seed is sowed, letting the fertilizer and grain fall together in the same drill row, but this should not be allowed with potassium salts or with acidulated bone meal, or any other acid phosphates because of the injurious effect of such fertilizers upon the germination of the seed. An end-gate seeder can also be used for applying bone meal, ground rock phosphate, potassium salts, or light applications (500 to 1,000 pounds) of ground limestone. If potassium is used it can be applied broadcast very rapidly with an end-gate seeder, and then the phosphorus can (in bone meal or ground rock phosphate) be applied through the fertilizer box at the same time the seed is put in, with no danger of injuring the seed and with practically no extra expense. Any of these materials can also be applied by hand very rapidly, and, if care is taken, very uniformly. A man can stand in a wagon (with a boy to drive) and he can spread any of these materials over twenty acres in a day. Last spring one man in Whiteside County spread potassium sulfate at the rate of 100 pounds to the acre over twenty-two acres of swamp land in less than one day's time, and the results obtained in the crop show that it was applied very satisfactorily.

For general farming in Illinois, there is absolutely no need of a ready mixed fertilizer. It costs the manufacturer from $4 to $8 a ton for mixing bone meal with potassium chlorid (or at least the mixed goods cost the consumer that much more than the raw materials). The manufacturer is frequently obliged to grind up rock or stones or some other worthless waste material and mix it with the plant food material which he puts in, in order to be able to put the price per ton down so that foolish farmers will buy it. Of course, if the farmer says he will buy "fertilizer," but he "won't pay more than $20 a ton for it," the dealer is bound to get him goods that he can sell for $20, or even for $15 a ton if necessary. Sometimes land plaster or gypsum (calcium sulfate) is used as the "filler," or "make weight." This material acts as a stimulant to the soil, causing it to give up some plant food and sometimes for a year or two to yield somewhat better crops, but it contains none of the valuable elements of plant food, and its action is simply more completely to exhaust the soil of its remaining stock of native fertility, finally to leave the land in even worse condition than before it was used. Acid phosphate such as acidulated bone meal, acidulated rock phosphate, and so-called superphosphates, all contain about 50 percent or more of gypsum, produced in the regular process of manufacture, besides the gypsum which is sometimes added as "make weight."

No general farmer in Illinois needs to purchase more than two elements of fertility. These are phosphorus and potassium. Bone meal will furnish the phosphorus and potassium chlorid the potassium, in the cheapest forms which are known to be available and without injurious effects on Illinois soils. Yet there are sold every year to general farmers in the United States more than a thousand different brands of fertilizers. Most of them contain more or less nitrogen (which costs the purchaser at least 15 cents a pound, but which he could get from the air for about 1 cent a pound); otherwise they have no value except for the phosphorus and potassium which they may contain. Some fertilizer manufacturers evidently prefer to have the farmer know nothing about soil fertility and fertilizers, excepting that their "Big Ox Brand," or their "Money Maker" or "Corn Grower" is the only and all sufficient fertilizer for all soils if not even for all crops. Some soils are deficient in nitrogen and consequently need to grow legume crops; some soils need phosphorus; and some soils have an abundance of both nitrogen and phosphorus (more than the most productive black prairie soils in the state), and yet are exceedingly deficient in potassium (see Table 4, page 20 of Circular No. 68). On the other hand, some crops require many times as much of one element as some other crops. (See Table 1, page 4, of Circular No. 68.)

It is a pleasure to state that, as a rule, the fertilizer manufacturers and dealers in Illinois are working in harmony with the University of Illinois to encourage the farmers in this state to try to understand what their soils need to increase the yields of the crops they grow, and I think farmers who desire to try phosphorus on their land will have no difficulty in obtaining pure bone meal from such trustworthy firms as Nelson Morris & Company, Union Stock Yards, Chicago, Armour Fertilizer Works, Swift & Company, or from several other companies located at the Union Stock Yards. Several of these companies, including the Armour Fertilizer Works, also sell pure potassium salts, such as potassium chlorid (sometimes incorrectly called "muriate" of potash) and potassium sulfate.

As a rule, not more than one of these two elements, phosphorus and potassium, is needed on the soils of the state, although it may be that both elements can be purchased with profit for use on some southern Illinois soils.

The element phosphorus can be purchased for about 12 cents a pound in bone meal, or for about 3 cents a pound in ground rock phosphate. Good steamed bone meal and good ground rock phosphate each contain about twelve to thirteen pounds of phosphorus in 100 pounds of the material. The element potassium can be purchased for about 6 cents a pound in potassium chlorid. One ton of commercial potassium chlorid (containing about 80 percent of pure potassium chlorid and 20 percent of sodium chlorid, or common salt) contains about 840 pounds of the element potassium, which, at 6 cents a pound, makes it worth $50.40. It can be bought from Chicago dealers for about $50 a ton. Of course freight charges from Chicago must be added to the Chicago price.

The fertilizer law of Illinois requires that every bag of fertilizer which is sold in this state must bear a printed label stating the percentage of the different elements of fertility which it contains, and any farmer can tell from the printed guarantee just what a bag of bone meal contains. Thus, if the label guarantees the goods to contain 12½ percent of phosphorus, this means twelve and a half pounds of the element phosphorus in 100 pounds of the bone meal, or 250 pounds of phosphorus in one ton of the bone meal. If the phosphorus is worth 12 cents a pound, such bone meal as this would be worth $30 a ton. Good steamed bone meal contains from 12 to 13 percent of phosphorus and is usually sold at retail for about $28 a ton at almost any place in Illinois.

In this connection, it may be said that the statements printed upon bags of fertilizers are commonly quite complicated. For example, the following statement may be given as the guaranteed analysis of a fertilizer:

Name, "**Soluble Ammoniated Bone and Potash.**"

ANALYSIS.

Available nitrogen .... 1.25 to 2.50
Available ammonia .... 1.50 to 2.75
Available phosphorus .... 4.00 to 5.50
Available phosphoric acid .... 9.00 to 12.00
Equal to bone phosphate .... 20.00 to 26.00
Total phosphorus .... 6.75 to 8.50
Total phosphoric acid .... 15.75 to 18.50
Equal to bone phosphate .... 34.25 to 42.50
Soluble potassium .... 1.50 to 3.25
Soluble potash .... 1.75 to 3.50
Equal to potassium sulfate .... 3.25 to 6.50

Now, what does this all mean? To understand this analysis, the farmer should first cut out everything except the minimum guarantee of the elements, nitrogen, phosphorus and potassium, as indicated by the bold-face type. To say that a fertilizer contains from 4.00 to 5.50 percent of phosphorus does not necessarily mean that it contains more than 4.00 percent, and 4.00 percent is really all that is guaranteed. Furthermore, it should be borne in mind that the law allows (and very properly so) a deficiency of 1 percent below the guarantee before it is considered positive evidence of fraud, consequently, the fertilizer may contain only 3 percent of phosphorus, under a guarantee of 4.00 to 5.50 percent, and still be within the limits of the law. It should be stated, however, that goods from trustworthy manufacturers are usually up to their minimum guarantee. Nevertheless it will be seen that a fertilizer might be sold with this long statement of the analysis as given above and complying strictly with the law, it might nevertheless contain only the following percentages (or pounds per hundred):

Available nitrogen... .25
Available phosphorus 3.00
Total phosphorus 5.75
Soluble potassium .... .50

Now, it should be understood that the farmer does not need to purchase nitrogen, and consequently that item should not be considered as adding to the value of the fertilizer. Even if he did wish to buy nitrogen this amount, .25 percent, is less than is contained in a normal fertile soil. In other words, the ordinary black prairie soils of Illinois are worth as much a ton for a fertilizer as the nitrogen value of a ton of any commercial fertilizer which contains only .25 percent of nitrogen and which may be lawfully guaranteed to contain 1.25 percent (some peaty soils found abundantly in Illinois contain about 3.50 percent of the element nitrogen). Many soils in the state also contain more than .50 percent of potassium, and a fertilizer should not be considered much more valuable because it contains ten pounds of potassium in a ton (either potassium chlorid or potassium sulfate contains 800 pounds of potassium in a ton (see Circular No. 68, pages 4 and 11).

In this connection attention is called to the fact that fertilizers are frequently labeled "Dissolved Bone," "All Soluble Bone," etc., which are not made from bone meal at all, but from acidulated rock phosphate. As rock phosphate contains a small amount of potassium, perhaps .5 percent, and as the sulfuric acid used in manufacturing acid phosphates usually contains a small amount of nitrogen, a plain acid phosphate could be made which would conform to the above long statement of analysis within the letter of the law, but the farmer should immediately reduce such a statement to

Available phosphorus .... 4.00 percent.
Total phosphorus .... 6.75 percent.

and the absolute guarantee is practically only

Available phosphorus .... 3.00 percent.
Total phosphorus .... 5.75 percent.

This means that one ton of this fertilizer contains sixty pounds of available phosphorus worth 12 cents a pound, or $7.20, and fifty-five pounds of insoluble phosphorus worth not to exceed 3 cents a pound, or $1.65. Thus this fertilizer would be worth $8.85 a ton. Of course it ought not to be used on Illinois soils, because of the fact that it is an acid phosphate and, so far as we have yet learned from our soil investigations, the soils which need phosphorus are already too acid, and consequently we advise farmers against the use of acid phosphates. We also strongly recommend that they do not buy mixed fertilizers.

If phosphorus is needed (as it is on many soils in the state) buy fine ground bone meal (either raw bone, pure bone, or steamed bone, the last preferred) and apply it in moderate quantities, say 200 pounds an acre a year, or buy ground rock phosphate and apply at least 500 pounds an acre a year in connection with legumes or manure or both.

If potassium is needed, buy potassium chlorid or potassium sulfate and apply 50 to 100 pounds an acre a year. The first application on lands which are very deficient in potassium (as some of the swamp lands) should be about 200 pounds for the most profitable returns. By reference to page 4 of Circular No. 68, it will be seen that the grain and stover for 100 bushels of corn require seventy-one pounds of potassium. It would take about 175 pounds of potassium chlorid or potassium sulfate to furnish seventy-one pounds of the element potassium. Of course the roots of corn also require potassium.

If any one prefers to pay $16 to $17 a ton for kainit, containing 10 percent of potassium, than to pay $50 to $55 a ton for potassium chlorid, containing 42 percent of the element potassium, of course he has the privilege of paying about 8 cents a pound for potassium and of handling four tons of material instead of one.   Incidentally he pays the freight on three tons extra of common salt and other worthless material contained in the kainit, which is shipped all the way from the potash mines of Germany.

We especially recommend fine ground steamed bone meal for phosphorus and potassium chlorid for potassium.

SUMMARY OF BULLETIN No. 88.

The results thus far obtained from the soil investigations reported in this bulletin certainly justify drawing some very definite conclusions. The amounts which are mentioned as the price received for raising an acre of wheat is for seed, labor, use of tools, cost of threshing and marketing.   The interest on the investment (including the original land value and the added stock of fertility of somewhat permanent character), the total cost of annual soil treatment, and full payment for all fertility removed in the total crops (including nitrogen, which is really also covered by the cost of legume treatment allowed in the expense of annual treatment) have all been provided for outside of these net amounts which remain to pay for raising an acre of wheat.   Furthermore the value of the straw has not been considered, although the fertility which it contains has been provided for.   The price of wheat has been counted at 60 cents a bushel, which is surely conservative.   It is believed that the results reported are thoroughly trustworthy.

First.   Legume treatment for this soil is profitable as compared with no treatment.   Legume treatment alone increased the amount received for raising an acre of wheat from 88 cents to $1.42, and when the legume treatment was omitted from plot 8 (see plot 10), the amount received for raising an acre of wheat decreased from $11.88 to $10.15, making a reduction of $1.73 in the profits, even after allowing $1 for the expense of the legume treatment, and not taking into account the fact that the effect of the legume treatment will last more than one season.

Second.   Manure made on the farm can be applied to the soil with marked profit.   (The untreated plot paid only 88 cents for raising an acre of wheat, while the manured plot paid $3.57.)

Third.   Moderate applications of ground limestone to acid soils give evidence of marked improvement in the growth of legumes, but more data are necessary to determine fully the extent of this improvement.

Fourth.   The application of phosphorus is very profitable soil treatment.   (It should be applied only in connection with manure or legume treatment, unless the soil is already well supplied with nitrogen and organic matter.)   Applied with legumes and lime, the phosphorus increased the amount received for raising an acre of wheat from $2.73 to $7.30.   When applied with manure the increase was from $3.39 to $8.30.

Fifth.   Potassium has also been applied with profit especially when used in connection with legumes and phosphorus, the amount received for raising an acre of wheat having been increased from $7.30 (legume, lime, phosphorus) to $11.88 (legume, lime, phosphorus, potassium) by the addition of potassium, making an increased profit of $4.58.   (Phosphorus made $4.57.)   It should be understood that the use of potassium without phosphorus would undoubtedly result in loss on nearly all Illinois soils (swamp soils excepted).

In this connection attention is called to the effect of tile drainage in supplying potassium.   As a matter of fact, practically all of the soils of the state (swamp and sand soils excepted) contain large supplies of potassium in the subsoils, say between twenty and forty inches below the surface.   Tile drains laid at a depth of forty inches permit the excessive soil water to pass off quickly thus causing the soil to become more porous and allowing the air to enter to encourage nitrification and the liberation of plant food from the subsoil.   The plant roots are encouraged to grow deep into the soil and thus obtain potassium which they could not obtain if the subsoil was waterlogged more or less of the time during the season.

The results already obtained in support of such a theory are very meager and somewhat conflicting, and more data are needed and are being obtained as rapidly as possible.   However, in view of the facts, first that applications of potassium have markedly increased crop yields on this type of soil, and second, that the subsoil is actually rich in potassium, it seems worth while to call attention, tentatively at least, to the data given in the preceding tables indicating that tile-drainage may perhaps be just as effective and more economical as a means of supplying potassium to the growing crops, altogether aside from the other marked benefits which tile-drainage produces.

By referring to Table 2 it will be seen that results are reported from our tile-drained soil experiment field at Odin.   The tile-drainage increased the yield of oats in 1902 from 16.7 to 19.2 bushels, where legume treatment, lime, and phosphorus had been applied, and in 1903 the tiled plot with this treatment yielded 13.4 bushels of wheat, while the corresponding untiled plot yielded only 5.8 bushels.   It will also be noticed that the application of potassium increased the yield of wheat from 5.8 to 14 bushels on untiled land, while on the tiled land the increase due to the application of potassium was only from 13.4 to 15.2 bushels.   Potassium benefited the oats on the untiled land but it appears even to have reduced the yield on the tiled land.   These results indicate quite strongly that tile-drainage at Odin may enable the crops to get about

PLATE 7.—WHEAT CROP WITH NO TREATMENT: ORDINARY FIELD ON GRAY
SILT IN ST. CLAIR COUNTY: ADJOINING FIELD SHOWN IN PLATE 8.

PLATE 8.—WHEAT CROP AFTER 40 LOADS WHEAT STRAW HAD BEEN LEACHED
AND BURNED OFF: ADJOINING FIELD SHOWN IN PLATE 7.

as much potassium as they need. Of course more data are needed before final conclusions can be safely drawn.

In conclusion it should be stated that the season of 1903 was one of the worst for the wheat crop which has been known in southern Illinois for many years. It seems fair to expect more marked results and larger yields from our soil experiment fields in a normal season.

Special attention is called to the very evident fact that the poor season is not altogether to blame for the poor crop of wheat. We can realize this better when we remember that in the same field of wheat at Cutler one plot produced 6 bushels an acre and another 26.8 bushels; at Odin one plot produced 0.5 of a bushel an acre and another plot 15.2 bushels. Furthermore, it was possible to find some good patches of wheat almost everywhere throughout the wheat growing area of southern Illinois. For example, plate 7 shows the wheat crop growing in an ordinary field on the farm of Philip Postel located on the gray silt soil in St. Clair County, while plate 8 shows the wheat crop growing on "strawed potato" land immediately adjoining this field. The two crops as indicated in the photographs were growing within twelve feet of each other. The season was the same for each and the soil was originally exactly the same type and formerly of the same productive capacity.

Why is this difference? In answer, let me call attention to the facts that this excellent plot had grown potatoes in 1901, that these potatoes had been covered with some forty loads of wheat straw to the acre; that this straw had lain on the ground for a year, and what had not rotted or leached out during that time had been burned and the ashes containing the lime, phosphorus and potassium, not already leached out, had thus been added to the soil in readily available form.

By referring to Table 1, page 4, Circular No. 68, it will be seen that forty tons of wheat straw would thus supply to the soil eighty pounds of phosphorus and 680 pounds of potassium. That is two pounds more phosphorus and 560 pounds more potassium than we have applied to our soil experiment fields during two years' time, besides the straw must have furnished a considerable amount of nitrogen (leached into the soil before it was burned). This object lesson, picked up in passing the field, serves to confirm strongly the results obtained on the experiment fields and emphasizes the tremendous importance of plant food in crop production.

Note.—This bulletin is hurried to publication with the thought that it contains information of very great value to those southern Illinois farmers who will be sowing wheat within a few weeks. It is earnestly suggested that they begin at least in a small way to build up a piece of land and thus obtain some definite knowledge from their own farms. At least try 200 pounds of bone meal on half an acre either in connection with farm manure or where legumes have been grown, and observe the results for two or three years.

CPSIA information can be obtained
at www.ICGtesting.com
Printed in the USA
BVHW091507191118
533509BV00029B/3245/P